# Will You Remember?

Story by
## Bonnie E. Crowe

Drawings by
## Alyssa Charlotte

*Published by*

**Bonnie Crowe**


ISBN: 979-8-218-07662-7


Copyright © 2022 by Bonnie Crowe




Story by Bonnie Crowe
Drawings by Alyssa Charlotte

Layout by Gary A. Rosenberg
www.garyarosenberg.com


Printed in the United States of America

*This book is dedicated to Bonnie's two sons, Steven and Michael.*

*The brothers were best friends from the day Michael was born, and they remained that way despite Steven's many hospitalizations. Michael remained a great source of comfort for Steven, whom he dearly loved. His ability to show compassion began in his early childhood. Michael and his wife, Janet, brought three brilliant and happy children into the world. The children's artwork is featured in this book.*

*Steven, unfortunately, died too soon after suffering for 38 years from a debilitating autoimmune disease. Steven's second home was Egleston Hospital and Emory University Hospital. His sense of humor, combined with his brilliant mind, made him a mentor for others and an instant friend to strangers. His goal was to finish his PhD at Emory University, but his pain was more than God would permit. His loss leaves a permanent void in Bonnie's life. If you know Bonnie, then you would know Steven. He emulated her father.*

*On a side note, all of the story illustrations were done by Michael & Janet's daughter Alyssa Charlotte when she was only seven years old, with additional contributions by Andrew and Adrian (all three were inspirations for this book).*

Will you remember the day you were born,
wrapped in a blanket so soft and warm?

4

Will you remember your beautiful crib,
your cozy jammies, your cute little bib?

Will you remember the way you wiggled,
you were so cute you made us giggle?

Will you remember waking at dawn,
enjoying your day until it was gone?

Will you remember your very first steps,
little hands reaching and trying your best?

Will you remember your first birthday cake,
icing on your fingers, and pictures to take?

1st bday
1st
11

B
B
A
A
C

Will you remember discovering rocks,
sniffing flowers and stacking your blocks?

Will you remember your favorite toys,
from sponges that paint to trucks that make noise?

16

Will you remember the first foods that you ate,
with fingers, a spoon, and your very own plate?

Will you remember planting a tree,
digging in dirt, and setting worms free?

Will you remember the waves on the beach,
chasing the foam that tickled your feet?

Will you remember running around,
spinning and jumping and falling down?

Will you remember the sweet lullabies,
a nighty-night kiss while closing your eyes?

Will you remember the joy and the love
you brought to your family and those up above?

**YES, YOU WILL—**

when you are holding your own little one!

Artist:
Grandson
Andrew Sidney
(Age 13)

Artist:
Granddaughter
Alyssa (Age 15)

Artist:
Granddaughter
Alyssa (Age 10)

Artist:
Granddaughter
Alyssa (Age 13)

Artist:
Granddaughter
Alyssa (Age 12)

Artist:
Grandson
Adrian Michael
(Age 11)

# About the Author

**Bonnie Crowe** was born in the steel mill town of Aliquippa in Western Pennsylvania. Her father was in the home furnishings business and her mother was a kindergarten teacher for the Aliquippa School System. She attended Kent State University and graduated with a bachelor's degree in Early Childhood Education from Point Park College.

After moving to Atlanta, Bonnie received her master's degree in Early Childhood Education from Mercer University. Her teaching experience with children includes Pittsburgh City Schools, Head Start, Pittsburgh Area School for the Blind, Western Psychiatric Institute (internship with Fred Rogers, which was instrumental in developing her appreciation of children's artwork), and Atlanta City Schools. All these teaching experiences were at the preschool or early elementary education level.

After having her first child, Bonnie began teaching evening adult education courses for childcare instructors at Dekalb Technical Institute and was a lead instructor for all evening classes for 14 years.

In 1985, her students—who consisted of teachers, directors, and owners of childcare centers—talked her into coming onsite to their facility to train and educate their staff. Eventually, building through word of mouth, Bonnie was able to schedule sufficient classes to make this a full-time profession. She developed an onsite training company, working throughout metro Atlanta and her home state of Georgia. She also has trained staff in Florida, Alabama, North Carolina, and South Carolina.

Bonnie is currently president of a childcare consulting company with the goal of training childcare teachers and keeping them informed of all laws and research in the industry. She is a member of NAEYC and serves on various committees to improve the level of training in Georgia.

On a personal note, Bonnie has a loving and supportive husband along with two sons and three grandchildren. She loves her immediate and extended family, Her interests are music (from classical to soul, especially Motown), golf, exercising, and meeting and forming lasting friend-ships with diverse groups of people. This is her trademark and her heritage. Note the multicultural theme in the drawings created by her granddaughter. Acceptance of religious, racial, and ethnic backgrounds has been natural since childhood. Her parents raised her in a diverse community and she has successfully passed this on to her own sons and grandchildren.